Name Dropping

The Cedar Bar in the 1950s

And Short Story:
"I Love You and Isn't That What Counts?"

Hiag Akmakjian

riverrun

Jackson Pollock

ABOUT THE THIRD OR FOURTH TIME I saw Jackson Pollock he blocked the front door of the Cedar Bar and demanded to know why I wanted to go to a fucking shit hole like this.

He was obviously smashed, his normal state when not working, and I could see that as I was approaching the bar. It was a pleasantly cold winter night and he was standing in the thick falling snow peering squint-eyed through the tiny window of the red door of the Cedar Bar. In the quiet side streets of Greenwich Village the few parked cars were blanketed and the air so hushed you could actually hear the soft sighing sound the wet snowflakes made as they came floating past your ears.

Monday night was Jackson Pollock night, and once the regulars caught on that that was when Pollock showed up, Monday nights became as crowded and popular as weekend nights. He would come in from Springs, near East Hampton, at the eastern tip of Long Island, and detrain at Penn Station, nattily dressed – well-shined shoes, neat suit, spiffy tie and – of all things – a derby. From the station he would taxi uptown for his fifty minutes with his shrink, and then, with breaks at favorite watering holes, work his way down Manhattan to the Cedar Bar, where by evening he would arrive shit-faced and walking in with such controlled casualness you could clearly see he was already half-drunk.

Now, out in the hushed snowfall, I tried to go around the blockade. He had a mean look and seemed determined not to let me go by. As Pollock peered intently through the tiny window and snowflakes floated around his head it reminded me of a poetic scene in a Japanese film. Over his shoulder I could see John the bartender scowling behind the beer taps and wagging his head in wide swings back and forth. He respected Pollock and who he was but had lost all tolerance for his bingeing craziness. The Cedar Bar was a friendly neighborhood bar and John, co-owner with Sam, wasn't about to let some drunk spoil things. He felt protective of people who were just beginning to frequent the place for a meal, a habit John encouraged. The restaurant, only slightly better than a hash joint, was not the

Cedar Bar's strong point and did not show a profit and possibly never would, but that was beside the point. It was a nice quiet place to have an inexpensive meal and spend an evening, and Pollock had a way of annoying women, who to him, whether accompanied or not, were fair game. He would slide into the booth of a couple quietly having dinner and tell the man to get lost as he beamed a seductive smile at the startled woman shrinking from him. John, who even in the best of circumstances had strict rules about decency in barroom behavior, especially with respect to women, would swing into enraged action and throw Pollock out.

The two of us standing outside now, Pollock could see John at the beer taps, his expressive Polish face trying for a menacing look, while jabbing his index finger toward the door and yelling.

"I don't care who you are, Jackson – you're out! And don't ever come back! Out!"

I saw my chance and slipped around Pollock and went in past John violently muttering behind the bar and swiping a plastic spatula across the sudsy top of a beer, guillotining it.

"You're eighty-six, Jackson! Out!"

But Pollock, sad, mean, pitiably likable, knew his man and stood waiting for the change of heart that would come. As it undoubtedly would.

And sure enough, after a while John, looking disgusted with himself at caving in again, yelled toward the door: "Okay, okay, but this is the last time, Jackson. And I mean it this time!"

Gratefully Pollock crept in practically on tiptoes to communicate good intentions and politely ordered a cold bottle of Pabst Blue Ribbon. After a first long pull from the uptilted neck, he wiped his mouth with the back of his hand in Wild West cowboy style and smiled amicably at his old pal John.

But to old pal John a truce was merely a truce, not a peace treaty.

"Okay, Jackson," he said, "take it easy now. Just take it easy."

Artists' Hangout

A FRIEND HAD TOLD ME about the place: a bar in Greenwich Village where all the real artists went.

It was the early 1950s and I was just back from Paris where for three years of the G.I. Bill I had passed pleasant days painting nude women at the Académie de la Grande Chaumière and fun evenings in the company of these women, now dressed. in the Montparnasse cafes that had been made famous to Americans by lost-generation expatriates.

The friend who had told me about the Cedar Bar described it as a "dump". It was on University Place just off 8th Street, and I should go over for a look, he said. After the Dome, the Deux Magots and the Flore, and the Closerie des Lilas, with their sidewalk tables and colorful umbrellas on wide boulevards, the Cedar Bar looked as gloomy and forlorn as I imagined a third-class waiting room on some rural Balkan railway line would look.

I met Franz Kline there one afternoon, recognizing him from a photo in Art News. We were alone at the bar and I said hi and told him how much I admired his painting "Chief" then hanging at the Museum of Modern Art. He was waiting for DeKooning to go uptown together to see some art show. We talked and became friends.

I was living quite near the Cedar Bar and began going there often and saw Kline a few more times and met the other artists and eventually nearly all of them – occasional drop-ins like Adolf Gottlieb, Jacob Lawrence, Ad Reinhardt, Barnett Newman, Larry Rivers, Joan Mitchell, Louise Nevelson – many women – and of course the regulars, by then already a little famous, Willem DeKooning, Mark Rothko, Philip Guston.

In Paris I had been asked about Pollock by Alice B. Toklas, whom I had met one day on the rue de Buci with a Spanish artist friend I was studying with privately. Introduced to "Mees Toe-KLAHSS" I admired her handsome hooked nose and the well-defined moustache darkening her upper lip. She was clutching a string shopping sac with carrots and bearded leeks poking through the wide cotton mesh as the three of us stood talking among the vegetable and cheese stands in the crowded market street. She was still in mourning for her lover Gertrude Stein, dead less than a year, and under her cropped Joan of Arc haircut, like an overturned bowl on her head, her dark sunken eyes dolefully sized up this new generation of art student from the States. She sounded patronizing and sour about the artists in New York and asked if Pollock was an out-and-out phony who flung paint on walls or was he maybe just psychotic.

She had no use for what was happening in America. America was the past. Paris was the leader in art.

Louie Holding the Fort

THE CEDAR BAR'S DAYTIME BARTENDER was Louie, a short worried-looking Greenwich Village Italian-American with a facial tic whose intermittent rhythm gave his eyes a nervously happy twitch. Nothing much ever happened on his shift, and he looked for ways to pass drowsy afternoons. On one particularly slow afternoon, I saw him seize a giant Hebrew National salami and, holding it between his legs, puff out his chest like a schoolboy having fun and strut down the duckboards behind the bar proudly bouncing the salami up and down in front of him to the macho amusement of the two lonely male drinkers at the bar.

One daytime customer was an attractive former athlete, now in her forties, who would appear wearing a maroon T-shirt with white lettering: "Olympic Drinking Team". Another was Betty, a bosomy, no longer young matron who after downing a few beers would remove a hefty breast from inside her dress and lovingly plop it on the bar, crooning to the flattening globe as if it were a baby. Each time Louie saw her hand reach into her blouse he shook his head and with a nervous smile urged her to put that thing away, for god's sake, and as she lovingly returned the breast to its place, the tic in Louie's eyes would spasm into rapid-fire blinks, and a grin would betray his happiness at the way the afternoon was turning out.

I got to know her. Her husband had walked out on her just before the birth of a baby, a boy who had lived six days. Carefully placing the body in a shoebox, she took the ferry to Staten Island and buried it under a lilac bush. She milked herself for several days to make her breasts stop aching, telling me all this the first time I met her and then asking the story of my life.

"We all have a story," she said as prompt.

11

John and Sam

THE TWO YOUNG OWNERS of the Cedar Bar were John Bodnar, who had been a window washer before the war, and his brother-in-law Sam Diliberto, who had been a butcher. They decided after they were discharged from the army that they wanted to own a bar that appealed to a respectable, middle-class clientele. The two used the G.I. Bill to attend a bartending school that formed, as Sam liked to describe it, graduate mixologists. Sam was the more adventurous of the two and took pleasure in making Cuba Libras, Singapore Slings, Sidecars, Stingers, Gimlets, and tropical rum concoctions topped with pink umbrellas and chunks of fruit around the rim – a professional accomplishment we had to take on faith because to my knowledge none of these drinks were ever served at the Cedar Bar.

Taking their savings out of the bank, John and Sam bought the Cedar Street Tavern and even retained the nineteenth-century name derived from the bar's original location at the bottom of Manhattan. They were saddened when their hope of attracting a bourgeois clientele didn't pan out. The customers who dropped in were mainly the painters on their way home from attending a meeting at their new Club and not the kind of drinker who would ever have need of a mixologist. They were a beer and whiskey crowd, which left Sam feeling the way a world-famous pianist might feel at a concert in Carnegie Hall if asked to perform his interpretation of chopsticks.

It didn't take long for John and Sam to lose their anxiety about mortgage payments and begin to feel an urge to improve the decor of the bar if they wanted the young enterprise to thrive and attract a nice money-spending bourgeois clientele. It made them happy to know that the Cedar Street Tavern as the hangout of artists was getting frequent mentions in places like The New York Times and Art News and its fame was spreading along with the fame of its clientele. The artists, egalitarian to the core, invited John and Sam to their 57th Street openings, and soon the partners were finding themselves drawn into the Manhattan art world. Awed by the artists' connections to uptown classiness, Sam came up with the idea of making the Cedar Bar an art bar by decorating the walls with samples of their work. ("You know, make it your bar" – friendly Italian-handsome smile.) He thought it would be pleasant if you looked at, say, a Pollock and a DeKooning on the wall as you sipped your drink. The painters thought otherwise, and when Pollock and DeKooning – and Rothko, Kline, Motherwell and the other artists – got wind of his proposal they threatened to find a new bar to go to. They wanted to keep the Cedar Bar the nice bare third-class-waiting-room dump they had always liked and where no tourist was ever tempted to drop in. DeKooning's approval of the premises was categorical and heartfelt: it was, he said, a "no atmosphere" bar. And wanted it kept that way. The last thing the artists wanted was to have it become a pretty Greenwich Village tourist spot. As compromise, they suggested Sam put up small prints of the moon glowing over the Bay of Naples, or red-coated English fox hunters and beagles outside a village pub, or four dogs at a card table playing poker – little framed things no one would bother to look at.

The impasse was broken when John suggested he hang up a handsome deep-sea fish he had caught. His new income had enabled him to realize his dream of being an amateur angler, and on a recent trip to Florida he had caught a beautiful long sleek colorful sailfish and had had it stuffed and mounted. It went up now high above the bar's cash register, and seeing the sailfish's arched body leaping from the sea in all its colorful and shiny shellacness, everyone gave it a thumb's up. Sam never stopped hoping that someday the artists would hang some of their work around the walls and make the Cedar Street Tavern an artistic bar, but except when he was among close friends, he knew better than to ever bring the subject up again.

The Club

THE CLUB, ON 8TH STREET around the corner from the Cedar Bar, was the top floor of an abandoned tenement. The walls of the three flights of stairs to the top were covered by old eroding paint jobs that combined to look like some third-stage skin disease in an illustrated medical textbook. The Club was opposite the Art Cinema, the Village movie house that showed good foreign films and had an apartment over its marquee inhabited by a very young couple who were either world-class exhibitionists or just beginning their honeymoon and not yet concerned about things like drapes.

The painters of the Cedar Bar founded the Club in 1947 in homage to the Armenian-American artist Vostanik Manoog Adoyan, known by his adopted name Arshile Gorky. Until then the painters had informally gathered at the Waldorf Cafeteria on Sixth Avenue and 8th Street until management made them feel uncomfortable for spending an evening at a table for four over one cup of coffee. This extreme frugality was a hangover from Depression days, whose effects lingered among artists, who might not have survived without FDR's Works Progress Administration's mural programs for artists. The Club gave them a place to discuss their work or hear talks by guests from MoMA who felt that one way to keep in touch with art movements was by hobnobbing with the artists. After the meeting, painters who didn't have to get up early to go to some job would stop off at that little bar around the corner.

As the fame of the artists grew, the Cedar Bar caught on as hangout. On nights when painters dropped in, the character of the place changed, especially Friday nights, when it got so mobbed that if you arrived between eleven in the evening and one in the morning you had to squeeze through bodies to enter. Fifty to a hundred painters, along with friends and lovers, packed themselves three deep between the bar and the wall and everybody shouted to be heard. As the artists began enjoying critical attention, women art lovers from the Upper East Side started showing up for flings, affairs and one-night stands with fame. Franz Kline, a frequent recipient of their favors, referred lovingly to these fashionable women as "name-fuckers".

Franz Kline

OF ALL THE PAINTERS who went to the Cedar Bar, I liked Franz the most. I liked him so much that I tried to like what he was doing in his paintings but succeeded only in admiring the ones with broad sweeping strokes reminiscent of Japanese calligraphy.

His language was as sparse as his paintings, a private way of speaking that would have been bizarre if written down but made perfect sense when you heard him speak it. "Involved" and "situation" were the principal words, with "that's got nothin to do with it" an all-purpose dismissive. One of his explanations would begin: "It has to get involved, because if the thinness of this line doesn't get involved with this black space here, you've got a situation that won't work."

There was sometimes so much involvement in situations and the expressive "that's got nothing to do with it" that I had to keep from laughing. But as strange as it was, his verbal shorthand was contagious. A friend of Franz's kept finding himself "involved" in various "situations" and explained once how the foreground in a photograph we were viewing was involved in a spatial situation with the background, which was the main reason the fucking thing worked. I asked about a tree over to one side. "Na, na," he said, "that's got nothing to do with it."

Franz was then living in his studio on Avenue B, and as a painting space (or "situation") it seemed a tight fit for the enormous canvases he had begun working on. During Hitler's war the abstract-expressionists had gazed at the iconic "Guernica" in its place of honor at MoMA and hankered to make "Guernica"-size paintings. Awed by it, and inspired also by some of Matisse's giant canvases and the impressive scale of Monet's water lilies (and encouraged to think big by art dealers, big paintings bringing in big prices), they began doing things on the grand scale. It was thrilling to blow up a tiny bit of scumbled paint in a late Monet landscape into something that took up the whole wall of a museum. And once these paintings began selling, the money temptation, coming after the prolonged deprivation of the Depression years, was understandably hard to resist.

Curious to see how he painted, I asked Franz one day if it would disturb him if I watched him while he worked and he assured me it would not. He might even enjoy talking while he worked. Wearing regulation paint-spattered pants and a workman's 59-cent blue-denim hardware-store shirt that got more and more comfortable with successive washings, he set to work.

In a small neat arrangement in a portion of wood floor that was as paint-speckled as a Pollock, there was a half-empty gallon of flat white paint bought from Behlen's paint supplies and two open smaller cans of black. Arranged almost like a still-life, a large house-painter's brush sat beside two empty cardboard pails, a Chock Full o' Nuts coffee can half-filled with turpentine, a grungy cookie sheet, a palette knife, a thick stick for mixing paint, an old sponge, and a pair of black workman's shoes partly coated in gobs of white.

As I watched Franz, he applied a black stroke in a broad sweep across the middle of the canvas. It looked like the ink sketch that was sitting on the floor. His way of painting was to make swift pen-and-ink sketches with a watercolor brush on pages that he then tore from the Manhattan Phone Directory. Then he more or less transferred one of these spontaneous sketches onto canvas.

Underneath that first stroke he added short black lines and stepped back and considered what he had done. Apparently something was not right. With a one-inch edging brush he separated two black areas with a wettish scumbling of white streak, inserting the white with gentle care. Clearing his throat, he stepped back again, lit a cigarette and stared at the work.

"Looks interesting," he commented.

He went to an old fridge back in an area of stretched canvases and studio odds and ends, and returned with two cans of beer and a church key. He punctured the cans open, handed one to me and took a sip from the other and looked at the painting again. The strong black-and-white "subject" that was emerging reminded me of his caricatures at the Minetta Tavern on MacDougal Street where he used to go in his days as a cartoonist.

As he painted he told me he was an admirer of John

16

Sloan's. "He really knew how to draw." Franz had studied art at Heatherley's, the conservative London art school where, he said, he really learned proper drawing. "Like if you drew a model with her knee bending, the knee had to be a real knee and you had to make it so that it was bending."

He wanted to know what I thought of French painters and whether the French liked what was happening in America. I told him they were not much impressed. They felt that American painters looked like they didn't know what they were doing. I remembered hearing a remark Franz made as a group of us were leaving the opening of a show at the Stable Gallery, on Central Park South. Walking out Franz commented to DeKooning on the unusual work in the exhibit we had just seen:

"Well, now, that's something we don't have to try."

He opened two more beers, passed one over and asked if I knew a sculptor he named. I said I knew him from Paris. He laughed.

"After I'm dead, he's going to claim he and I were good friends. We're not."

We talked about various things, and he told me stories of his life. He had been in a fight recently and said his eyes felt like "two piss holes in the snow." I had heard him use that phrase before and could tell he liked the image.

As I was wondering what fight he'd been in, he suddenly switched tracks and announced that a big problem in life was rent money.

"Forget buying on mortgage. Once you've got a fuckin mortgage, they've got you by the nuts. You get into a whole suburban mortgage situation and you might as well quit painting. A painter is somebody who says piss on all that and just paints. You have to not be able to see yourself as doing anything else. Of course there's always that rent situation, but for that, you get involved in doing house moving or house painting, the same as Bill" (DeKooning) "and me too. We've all done it. It's not a bad way to go."

He'd spent years painting before he began doing what he liked and concluded with: "It's when you stop giving a fuck that you're really getting into it."

When his first dealer reported that his paintings were selling for an astounding three hundred dollars each, Franz went back to retrieve an early canvas he had given to an old girlfriend. He said he didn't feel too marvelous about taking it back from her, but the affair had been a brief one and didn't mean much to either of them. And three hundred bucks was three hundred bucks.

"She took it OK. So I got it home and hung it up on the wall and looked at it for a couple days. Then I thought, fuck it, and returned it to her. She took it all very nicely."

He seemed fairly happy about where he was in life. Soon the price of his paintings began to rise to a few thousand dollars each and then made a big jump to ten thousand dollars as his fame attracted big-time collectors. One admirer asked his dealer where he could find this great painter Frank Klink – the name misread on one of Franz's paintings. Franz enjoyed that story and enjoyed even more hearing from Hedy Lamarr, who phoned him one day. Admirers felt that the big-name movie star of the thirties and forties was the most beautiful actress of them all. Her acting career had begun to wane but she was still popular and enjoyed a certain fame for her quips. ("American men, as a group, seem to be interested in only two things, money and breasts. It seems a very narrow outlook.")

She asked Franz if he would trade a painting of his for one she had collaborated on with a young painter friend who was her current lover. Franz, ever generous, happily made the swap. He liked her absence of bullshit and sententiousness, two commodities he was allergic to and enjoyed puncturing. The painter Milton Resnick once said to Franz: "There's more to life than just fucking, you know." To which Franz replied, "For example, there's fucking."

When the last beers were gone he thought we might go get involved with a few more down at the Cedar Bar. He liked the Cedar Bar, but it was really the city of New York that he loved. He had come here from Wilkes-Barre, Pennsylvania, which was all pizzas and parking, and his opinion was unambiguous.

"New York is what it's all about."

Marcus Rothkowitz

FRIENDSHIP WITH FRANZ WAS EASY. With Rothko you had to work at it and earn it. Rothko lived deep inside a friendly truculence with a sign outside reading "No Admittance". His slightly wall-eyed stare put people off, and if he was feeling down, he quietly pounced on anything you said. But after he had been surly and distant for a while, he eased up on you and became merely distant.

I no longer remember what reasoning led him to think I might make a good child minder for his daughter Kate, and now, thinking back, the idea does seem preposterous, but it really happened. We were having a beer at the Cedar and Rothko asked if I needed part-time work and wondered if I would consider babysitting his daughter Kate.

Possibly he made the suggestion for the sentimental reason that I had lived in Paris, which we had been talking about, or possibly it was that he liked it that I had Armenian roots and his great friend and teacher Arshile Gorky had been an Armenian. But by whatever path he arrived at suddenly popping the question, the offer was apparently serious and he invited me to dinner at his place, in the West Fifties, so that his wife, who had the deciding vote, could see if I was suitable. She was a very gentle person, he said. He was getting a little famous then, and I had fantasies about going down in art history as the child minder of Mark Rothko's daughter.

On the day of the appointment, after two or three warm-up beers at the Cedar Bar to kill time, I went uptown and met Mrs. Rothko. She was as gracious as Rothko had led me to believe she would be and we hit it off from the start. She had prepared an Italian lasagna dinner that we, Rothko and I, proceeded to wash down with an open gallon of table red that was so good that, chuckling and laughing, we opened another gallon.

Things went well as I remembered Rothko's advice to be sure to please his wife and engage her in conversation that I thought might interest her, particularly a life in art. Mrs. Rothko spoke with pride about her husband's work – she didn't ever call him Mark but always Rothko – and asked about art in Europe and the history of the Armenian people and the usual stuff about how terrible the Turkish genocide was, and Rothko inquired about the goodness of various vintages of French wines and their regional differences and the general crappiness of the wine you got in New York.

These discussions went on for quite some time and glasses kept being refilled, and around midnight I became aware that Mrs. Rothko had long ago disappeared, and then it was one in the morning, and as Rothko and I were discussing where there might be a place open that sold wine, Mrs. Rothko reappeared, and Rothko said well maybe we could continue this another time as his wife softly aimed me toward the door. I felt a small bump nudging me over the threshold into the hall – possibly it was the door closing behind me.

I didn't see Rothko for several days and when we met again, he informed me quietly that the interview had not gone as well as he had hoped and regretted that I would not be hired, but that was the way it was. Actually I felt glad for the little girl Kate, whoever she was. She would never know how close she had come to being in the care of a two six-pack-a-day beer-swilling nanny.

The Parties

FRANZ WAS MORE REGULARLY in attendance than any of the other painters of the Cedar Bar and at four a.m. closing time would order nightcaps up and down the bar for anybody who might still be there. John the bartender would line up a row of beers in front of each drinker and in conformance with the law lock the front door. He would allow an extra hour for the last beers to be guzzled down while behind the bar he did paper work, or whatever it was he did before calling it a night. Then he would shoo everybody out, "Time to go now, time to go, folks!"

Drinking up, our small group would leave, taxiing to an all-night deli uptown on Sixth Avenue where Franz knew he could buy after-hours beer to bring back to Washington Square Park for some predawn drinking. The standard taxis then were the spacious old Desoto behemoths with plenty of leg room for five passengers, two of them sitting on jump seats folded out of sight when not in use. Sometimes an illegal sixth passenger would be drunkenly smuggled aboard, with the driver ignoring the violation in his enjoyment of the laughter of the women perched, hip-hugged, on men's laps.

Weekend summer nights were party nights, and in the silence of the streets between Fourth Avenue and Avenue B from 8th to 10th Streets you could locate a party from half a block away by the mourn of a distant saxophone, and illegally bringing along a drink from the Cedar Bar for en-route sipping, you found the building and climbed up to the flat where dancers were flinging themselves around so energetically on the trembling floor that it was easy to imagine morning headlines about a tenement cave-in killing and injuring bohemian partiers.

On a good night it was possible to go to two parties in progress and choose the one with the greater sexual potential. Eighteen- and nineteen-year-old grass widows of the GIs in Korea were of a new generation that, missing sex and not always giving a damn what society thought of them, went to parties with the same hope for wild promiscuity as the men.

One muggy dog-day night, hearing the wonderful supercharged racket of a party as I passed the windows of Auden's ground-floor flat across from the baths on St. Mark's

Place, his apartment sublet while the poet was away, I wandered in to rooms of old painted walls and dust-caked bare wood floors that only a poet could call home.

I scooped up a glass of punch from a bowl on the floor of one of the rooms and went hunting for ice. As I picked up a discarded cube from the kitchen sink, I looked up and was taken by surprise. The building's design was of an earlier era when it was legal to have a large sash window separating the kitchen from the toilet. The window, which began at the top of the sink, was normally rendered opaque with a coat of paint but on this hot summer night was wide open. Standing at the sink and looking into the john I saw a woman peeing in a knee-squatting straddle over the bowl. I was surprised, then delighted, when she left and I saw another woman come in and do the same, and then another – apparently a queue was forming outside the john door. Each performed similarly, none of them sitting, all with one hand hiking up their dress and the other hand reaching up to adjust an undergarment, if they were wearing any, and, with a vacant stare, letting go. Enthralled, I enjoyed this private ritual, each time admiring the way the woman could hit the bowl with ballpark accuracy. The parade ended when a new arrival, apparently less smashed than the others, spotted the accidental voyeur and dropping her hem like a shot, straightened up and marched indignantly up to the face grinning in the window and slammed it shut.

Roast Duck

WHEN THE CEDAR BAR FIRST OPENED, its restaurant menu listed various kinds of fish but its principal offering was hamburger, euphemistically listed as hamburger steak. It was a big, flat pancake of low-grade chopped meat. Its price of sixty-five cents included French fries and one cup of coffee.

More attractive was the chef's special, duck à l'orange, but that was available only once a week. Sometimes the waiter, Albert, would serve the duck dinner no matter what you ordered and make the bill out for the hamburger steak. He was a plump middle-aged anti-Nazi German, a closet gay with a stubble-bearded face, and more friend to artists than waiter, and he took a maternal pleasure in seeing that artists who might be broke got good nourishing meals. He admired the refugee German artist George Grosz and could never forgive the Nazis for their treatment of so great a talent, and possibly it was with private thoughts of avenging Grosz's mistreatment that Albert took it on his own to serve painters the roast duck in place of hamburger steak. ("Vee are oudt of hom-boorger – vee haf goot duck tonight.")

The duck – forget Paris, and forget especially the Tour d'Argent – would have been at the very top of a cardiologist's list of forbidden foods. None of the duck's thick coat of blubbery protective winter fat was removed. Which had the incidental effect of making portions look plate-fillingly generous. And there was consensus that the l'orange element came out of a chef's half-gallon professional tin of factory marmalade liberally slathered on the roasted bird with a palette knife. Then, meal over and plates taken away, Albert made the bill out for one barley soup and one coffee per person, and in return asked only to be given a kiss – "Choost a little küss, ja?"

None of us ever küssed Albert, but that did not discourage him from serving roast duck dinners every time it appeared on the menu – until the day came when John's bookkeeper, doing a quarterly accounting, discovered anomalies between total dinners served and dollar amounts settled. That abruptly ended Albert's humanitarian efforts in artists' aid, and it remained a mystery to me what the chef in the kitchen must have been thinking during all those weeks when he kept noting the disappearance of duck dinners from the kitchen with nobody ever ordering them.

More Pissing

ONE EARLY DINNER AT THE CEDAR BAR arrived every evening at the same hour and squeezed always into the same two-person booth, opened an evening newspaper and read it as he sipped a martini, followed by a second and even more satisfying martini, and then a third and final martini as he ordered the daily special, which he chewed thoughtfully and slowly before slipping into a post-breastfeeding slumber. I observed in fascination as his eyes drooped and his cherubic face nodded in gentle bounces downward until his chin landed on his chest, where a strangled snore jolted him into groggy arousal. Then he was all business as he worked his girth free of the booth and stiff-jointedly toddled to his feet and, bearings regained, strode to the door like a man with a purpose in life. He got to the street with only one brisk bounce against the wall as the door shut behind him.

I think but am no longer sure that the lone diner was a lover of Dawn Powell's, the snub-nosed middle-aged novelist who would drop in at happy hour for a drink at the bar, not talk to anyone, look like she was writing in her head, pay up and leave. The literary critic Edmund Wilson was a champion of hers, and as it happened a journalist and critic I much admired for his measured views and leftist opinions and his expressive way with simple words. (I admired less but was all the same amused by his idiosyncrasy of offering praise with one hand while yanking it back with the other: "It was an unforgettable achievement, in a small way." "It had a certain purity, in a squalid way."

Inspired by his praise, I tried Powell's novel The Golden Spur, said to be about the Cedar Bar, and discovered it was more a case of Wilson's having a warm spot for an old flame, as he had for women writers and actresses he had dallied with.

Reading Wilson made me curious to see the dime-a-dance halls he described in one of his Depression-era articles, and I found an old hall on Fourteenth Street, just past Lüchow's Restaurant. Remarkably, it was still in business though shabby, its years of success well behind it. At a forlorn-looking booth in front, I bought a dollar's worth of tickets and went in to a small patch of a dance floor and empty tables in a vast, dark, high-ceilinged cavern. Over in a corner a five-piece band of black musicians was playing lifelessly for a dancing couple in the middle of the small barren dance floor. The man "dancing" was shorter than his obese partner, who looked like she was smothering him as they stood in one spot and rhythmically ground groin against crotch. At thirty-second intervals a cowbell went clunk clunk to announce the limit of a ten-cent ticket, although the band, its playing unconnected with the clunking, continued nonstop to the woman's squirming vigorously against the man's crotch.

Over at the side, another man sat at the one occupied table, sharing it with two women. The women had mammoth breasts, each incredibly the size and shape of a long summer watermelon. They were grotesque. One of the women – her teased hair built high and sprinkled with sparkles that caught the light – seeing me looking at her, said in a friendly voice: "How do you like my tits?"

She asked if I wanted to dance with her and indicated her female companion as an alternate, if I preferred, and asked if I'd like to buy "she and I" a drink. The only drinks in the place were paper cups of ginger ale. The man who had been sitting with the two women finished his drink and held the cup out to her with the request that she "put something sweet in it for me." She went to the women's room and returned with the paper cup partly filled with a pale amber fluid. I assumed his pleasure came from the mild aroma and from imagining the part of her anatomy where the cup had just been held.

I handed my unused tickets to the sparkly-haired one who had asked if I admired her tits and said good night. She wriggled a chubby handful of pudgy fingers at me and smiled in a sociable way.

"My name's Lucille," she said in a sweet voice.

"Good night, Lucille."

"G'night, hon," she said. "'N thanks."

On my way to the door I passed the couple on the dance floor still purposefully squirming, not there yet, and left wondering what the hell Edmund Wilson ever saw to draw him to a place like that. But maybe it was different in the twenties and thirties, when, who knows, possibly dime-a-dance halls had a certain purity, even if only in a squalid way.

Art and Pomposity

ARTISTS AT THE CEDAR BAR seldom liked to talk about painting, and some felt as Pollock did. He hated all talk about all art. Whatever an expert or curator had to say about art was by definition and ipso facto crap.

I could understand Pollock's scorn and even share some of his distrust. A column in The Nation by the art critic Clement Greenberg about a particular painting of Piet Mondrian's explained how the artist had judiciously chosen a particular set of colors in a painting, Greenberg saying that those colors would convey exactly the right emotional intensity. Which sounded fascinating until I read Greenberg's embarrassed retraction in the next issue. He apologized that actually the colors in the painting were not the ones he had so lovingly admired the week before – and there went their appropriateness for the right emotional intensity.

The new private language of the art critics of New York, talking about the boys in the Cedar Bar, was not always decipherable, and one day I understood why the artists never questioned the profound twaddle: it sounded complimentary to hear that "the logistics of the spatial dimensions do disservice to the events within the frame." Or that "forms with a catalytic force grow from ambiguous fountain heads." There seemed to be a kind of gentleman's agreement that such collections of words had meaning and there was something comforting about them. A painter reading that his work had a "referential dimension in its tonality" almost didn't care what it meant. It had a thoughtful sound and added distinction. Equally exhilarating was to read that "the evolving, inundating tones of the artist's palette shimmered the senses into an apprehension of emotions too submerged to be summoned by superficial imagery." Artists have always had an understandable hunger for appreciation, and even if they were not certain what the hell that meant, they ate it up.

Many of those successful painters who were not always happy with what they were doing began believing this high-velocity prose about their work and felt encouraged to go on. Praise, even when it sank into unintelligibility, was hard to give up. The artists whose work sold for the most money read the most pretentious declarations about their work. As their prices soared and dealers began playing as big a role in art as the artists themselves did, their paintings got the ultimate mark of distinction: they were declared "important". Soon the artists were making attempts of their own at fancy talk. When Grace Hartigan began a piece with "Wasn't it Gide who said . . . ?" she knew it would instantly place her in a class apart from the other Cedar Bar painters. And Mark Rothko, emulating the critics' manner, declared that "flat forms . . . destroy illusion and reveal truth", a remark that was lucidity itself compared with a later critic's explanation of a Rothko early painting of two nudes: "The logistics of the gaze infiltrate the work, suggesting inwardness and events beyond the frame. The shocked mien in 'Untitled' implies an unseen transgression. In another canvas two stares lead to opposite directions . . . an eerie condition of de-centering."

It left you a little in awe.

Writers and a Movie Star

THE GROWING FAME OF THE CEDAR BAR was now drawing poets to the noisy evenings, where painters and an art atmosphere were a pleasant backdrop for those who liked to write on the hoof. Frank O'Hara, in a booth with friends, wrote bits of poems as his friends gossiped and joked, adding barroom chitchat to a poem in progress if a phrase sounded like it might fit in rather nicely.

As a break from the San Remo and the Kettle of Fish on MacDougal Street, Allen Ginsberg showed up a few times, and one night Jack Kerouac, piss-eyed passing-out drunk, lying face sideways on a beer-sloshed shiny black tabletop, angrily repeated in a slurred monotone his apparently new discovery about women: "They're cunts, that's all they are . . . cunts . . . Just fucking cunts."

One night Elizabeth Taylor showed up – and shock! It was as if Picasso had just strolled in.

Passing through New York, Taylor had answered an ad by Ted Joans, a young bearded African-American poet who offered Rent-a-Beatnik tours of Greenwich Village. On his itinerary of the Village he brought Taylor to this hot new place where all the artists went, the Cedar Bar, and walking into a roaring crowd of Saturday night drinkers they headed toward the booths in the back and as they looked around the room the Cedar Bar fell into an unnatural silence. It was as if an audio switch had been thrown. People who would never admit they could be awed by a movie star gawked at her as she silently gazed at the roomful of faces staring at her, until, without speaking, she glanced at Joans to turn around and leave. The drinkers near the bar shrank against the wall to allow her squeeze room to pass them again, as her frightened eyes – authentically violet – contacted each mesmerized person she passed. Someone opened the door for her and as she stepped through, she glanced back at John, frozen in mid-gesture behind the bar, his lips parting as he did an abrupt down-and-up chop with his chin in acknowledgment of the courteous smile she flashed back at him. The unreal silence exploded into its former roar, the volume now even greater than before, as John's ashen face stared at the doorway where she had slipped into the night.

The Always-Longed-For Past

THE EXCITING EARLY DAYS of the Cedar Bar did not extend much beyond the decade of the fifties. By 1956 Pollock was already dead, having wrapped his car around a tree in East Hampton. Rothko would die a few years later: his marriage troubled, and after a diagnosis of aortic aneurysm, he overdosed on anti-depressants and was found with one bloody arm sliced open with a razor – the multiply determined death echoing his teacher Gorky's, who, his arm paralyzed in a car accident, hanged himself when informed he would soon be dead of colon cancer. DeKooning, the longest survivor of them all, lived to his alcohol-sodden nineties, and with his Alzheimer-senile brain started giving chunks of his huge pile of money away to anyone who said he needed some.

Franz one day stopped drinking: in his doctor's opinion his heart would give out if he did not. The thought of dying at fifty frightened him into a "sobriety situation" – and with his absence the Cedar Bar felt like just any other bar. Those who had seen him there on occasional afternoons and most evenings missed him, as they missed Rothko too, who occasionally stopped downtown following some midtown gallery opening, with a good pint or two of Hiram Walker already inside him. But Rothko never stayed. With a dour look he took in the bar for a while, saw no future in it and left. And I missed DeKooning, the blue-eyed Dutch charmer, breezing in and in lilting accent shouting affably, "Well, what say we have a lil drink?" as Sam, behind the bar, cheerfully resigned, poured out plain old rounds of beers and whiskey. And there was Philip Guston, coming in one afternoon, beautifully tanked up from some uptown function, looking in his tweeds like a classics professor at one of the Seven Sisters who had wandered into the wrong profession.

They were successful now, all money anxieties behind them. There was the amusing anecdote that a member of the Guggenheim Committee leaked word that if DeKooning applied, the Foundation would be happy to award him a Fellowship and some amount like $10,000 – possibly more. According to rumor, DeKooning had made $200,000 by September of that year and his accountant had advised him to hold sales down to avoid paying higher taxes, and when he heard the Guggenheim report, DeKooning cried: "Now they want to help me?" – and found himself in the rare and to him gratifying position of telling the Foundation to shove its grant up its ass sideways.

Then one day Franz was back again, and it was beers all round as he explained that death by alcohol was preferable to death by boredom. I saw him only once after that, a sunny afternoon, as he sat alone at the bar, looking in the prime of life, Pennsylvania-Dutch handsome, mustache trimmed, cheeks clean-shaven, wearing his dark pin-striped suit and an open-neck white shirt and stylish hat. It was his dressed-for-major-events outfit assembled from the little Third Avenue pawnshops buried behind dark doorways under the El. He was not back from some uptown opening but from visiting his wife Elizabeth, committed in a Long Island hospital. She had been a ballet dancer when he courted her in London during his student days at Heatherley's and, once married and moved to America, she had grown unhappy in New York and had sunk into "a schizophrenic situation." In the medical wisdom of the period, the condition was triggered by the couple's unrelenting depression over poverty. I sat next to Franz, neither of us saying much, Louie on duty, Louie quiet too – after his visits to Elizabeth, Franz was all yeah, no, nothing, hmm, well, yeah . . . wiped out. Beer untouched.

Franz died in 1963, aged fifty-one – a rheumatic heart. And just around that time the younger, not-yet-known painters of the Cedar Bar shifted loyalty to their generation's new hangout, Max's Kansas City, a crowded bedlam of a bar a few blocks north, just beyond Union Square. The years were passing and one by one the artists of the Cedar Bar were disappearing from view. The bar's best days were gone.

In recent retrospect the painters who frequented the Cedar have begun to be described as the "greatest generation in American art history," with DeKooning as "the great Dutchman" and leader, Franz a "heroic" painter, Pollock a "giant of modern art" and Rothko a "towering tragic" figure. Such epithets would have made Franz uncomfortable and maybe DeKooning too, though not Rothko and probably not Pollock. I could – though slowly – agree to or at least uneasily comprehend the growing idolatry of these men by talking myself into believing that there was some Promethean esthetic line running from Fra Angelico to Monet and passing now through DeKooning and Pollock –

but I had difficulty accepting the recent flowering of Western art in a Brillo pad and a Campbell soup can. There was growing now a New Acceptance in America, the esthetic premise that if art could be anything, then anything could be art. What the painters of the Cedar Bar had so wildly done in the 1950s began to be regarded as High Renaissance compared with the stuff coming out of Andy Warhol's factory of drug-happy beatniks. It had now become the era of Max's Kansas City, which was the new Cedar Bar and a "haunt" of "creative ferment" and "legendary meetings", as these things tended to be described in art histories. And out of that time and the period that followed would come comic book art, minimalism, conceptualism, Vasarely's illusions, field painting, photo realism, media spectacles, sound and light shows, and God knows what else, each new movement supplanting everything that had come before and unintentionally conferring on the Cedar Bar's Abstract Expressionists the retrospective look of modern Old Masters.

To those who had been alive during the Cedar Bar's so-called golden years, none of it seemed great then and certainly not golden. It wasn't even a time that might someday be yearned for. You would have had to be slightly mad to think that way – until one day memory does its number and you get ambushed.

• • •

I Love You and Isn't That What Really Counts?

I was expected for lunch at twelve-thirty but as I was leaving to go over, the phone rang with the call I had been expecting from the Journal about a photo assignment on Hoboken the paper had proposed. We got into a discussion over certain details, and just as I was about to hang up, the editor brought up a point about secondary rights and as a result I arrived late.

Mr. Sforza, beaming as always, was affectionate and cordial and said everybody must be starved by now and we should all sit down and eat.

"Do I hear any objections?"

"No objections from me," his wife said.

I had brought the antipasto, a special prosciutto I get over on Ninth Avenue in Manhattan whenever I happen to be in that part of town. Mrs. Sforza, wearing her robin's-egg-blue apron that said "No Frills - All Thrills," a recent birthday present from either Dom or Paul, her two sons, served the prosciutto with a slice of honeydew melon.

It was early fall but still summery enough for the table to be set outside the ground-floor kitchen in the backyard, which was just cement space behind the buildings. The yards were sectioned off by fences of waist-high unpainted planks that ran from the buildings to a back alley. You could see across many yards. Outside some of the kitchens were plants in pots, and at the back end of the Sforzas' yard there was a pear tree that looked gaunt. Despite the tree and the plants, or maybe because of them, the back area had a desolate look, but you didn't see that if you lived there. The people who lived there thought of it as nice quiet backyards in Hoboken.

"Good prosciutt' - the real thing," Mr. Sforza said. "Probably from Manziano's again, right?"

"Prosciutt'. Italians really understand ham," Mrs. Sforza said with feeling.

When we were finished with the antipasto, Mr. Sforza went inside and brought out the main dish, which he himself had prepared. He enjoyed cooking but only what he called "nuts and bolts" food: roasts, cutlets, steaks.

"Anybody here hate capon?" he asked with a grin.

He set the platter of roasted bird at his place on the table and inhaled its aroma.

"This's going to be good," his wife said happily.

He carved out sizable portions and put three pieces on three plates and next to each piece added a white mound of mashed potatoes. With the ladle he poked a crater into the centers of the mashed potatoes and ladled in gravy, then added a large spoonful of peas alongside, carefully forming an island of the peas. He passed each of us a full plate, set one down at his place and took his seat.

"There's plenty of gravy, so help yourself."

We began eating. He poured us Chianti from a straw-covered bottle and toasted everyone's health: "Salut!"

"Did you know that Hoboken is now the most densely populated city in the United States?" Mr. Sforza said. "When my grandparents first arrived here back in the twenties Hoboken was mostly empty lots with a few scattered houses. It was New York's seaport then. In fact even when I was a kid, just before the second war, it still had that empty look. Remember?" he asked his wife.

Mrs. Sforza nodded and said: "Frankie Sinatra was around then too. He lived just a few of blocks from here - before Old Blue Eyes became a movie star. Now they call him Francis."

"Right, old Blue Eyes. Probably if he had been born and raised in London," I said, "he would have been Sir Francis by now."

"In Italy," Mr. Sforza said, "they would have made him Saint Francis by now."

"They already have a Saint Francis," Mrs. Sforza said. "And he's still Frankie to me."

She winced and eased dentures from her mouth and slid them back in again - a flash of white and pink upper plate. She smiled shyly when she saw me noticing.

The Castellanos - my family -- and the Sforzas had been living next door to each other in Hoboken for so many years we were more like uncles and aunts and cousins than neighbors, and after my parents died, whenever I called up Mr. and Mrs. Sforza to ask if I could come by and have lunch with them, they always said sure, come on over. They already had grandchildren but the generation gap didn't bother them or me - I doubt that we even thought about it. I knew they missed their sons Dom and Paul, who had been my friends as we were growing up and who had married and moved away and had families of their own now. I visited Mr. and Mrs. Sforza out of habit but also I was aware, living next door to them, how alone they were most of the time. The sons and their wives and children visited as often as they could, but that was seldom more than once a year -- almost always for Christmas.

I liked Mr. and Mrs. Sforza, Mr. Sforza because he loved his wife unsentimentally. "You have a good wife," I once heard a friend say to him and Mr. Sforza said, "She's okay." "Just okay?" "Very okay." He confided to me later, in case I might wonder if there was some secret to his marital happiness, "She's a woman you have to adjust to." I said that made her sound difficult and I hoped he didn't mean it that way, and he laughed as though I were cracking some dumb kind of joke and said: "No, no, no, she's easy. It's an easy adjustment." Which left me in the dark. "In other words, she's okay," I said as a prompt, hoping he would build on that and say something different. "Very okay," he replied in agreement.

I especially liked Mrs. Sforza -- the quiet energy compressed in that small aproned frame and her old-world look: soft white hair drawn to a tight bun behind her head, as in a daguerreotype, "Peasant Woman, Abruzzi 1850." I liked her eyebrows too - very bushy and pure white, rising and falling almost comically as she listened intently to whatever you said.

The Sforzas usually asked for family news and I always went prepared. I told them about my mother's oldest niece Lucy, who had married a college traveler for Prentice-Hall because, she said seriously, he was gone most of the time and she liked the quiet. Everyone liked her husband but we knew what she meant.

"Ralph, Lucy's youngest son, just got accepted at Stevens."

"Little Ralphie?" Mrs. Sforza said. "Jesus."

"Is his health any better now?" Mr. Sforza asked.

"His health has always been fine," Mrs. Sforza said. "What does health have to do with it?"

"Right," he said. "I was thinking of Angela's kid, with the lung."

I told Mr. Sforza I thought the capon was excellent and he told me I was obviously a gumba to appreciate down-home cooking - "old-country down-home cooking." Also this was no supermarket capon, he said. He got this beauty at Keller's farm, up near Lake Hopatcong.

"You went to Keller's?" Mrs. Sforza asked.

"How do you think this thing got here - UPS?"

"You went back to Keller's after that remark about Italians?" Mrs. Sforza said.

"Oh that was just his humor. The Kellers are nice people, believe me."

"Hu-mor?" Mrs. Sforza turned to me: "He said, 'Italians are good decent folk - both of you.'"

Her husband laughed. "Get it? That's funny."

"I don't care about the humor part. It's the other part I don't like," Mrs. Sforza said. "'Good decent folk?' - you kidding, 'folk'? When was the last time his country had a Renaissance?"

"Aa, you don't get the point. Here, have some more peas. Let me give you some more potatoes."

Docilely she held out her plate and accepted the potatoes. I marveled how much she could put away for her size. She set the plate down in front of her and rubbing her knuckles against her cheek massaged the gums from the outside.

"I'm glad you come around once in a while," she said. "We always eat good, but we usually eat better when you're here - you know, pig out when there's company. When you're retired you pig out a lot."

"Eating is the hobby of old age," Mr. Sforza agreed.

"In Florida in old age they play shuffleboard. Up here we pig out," his wife said.

"Down there they pig out too, don't kid yourself."

"On frozen orange juice."

Mr. Sforza said he and his wife enjoyed our get-togethers, and he thought that one of the reasons I had been coming over more frequently in recent months was that I was unconsciously searching for my dead father.

Mrs. Sforza looked aghast. "Jesus, Marco, where were you raised, on a raft?"

My father, who had been a widower for a few years, died six months ago of stomach cancer.

"No, hey!" Mr. Sforza said to me earnestly. "I don't mean that's the only reason you come over. And no disrespect. It's just that you're also looking for your father. You know how dogs and horses go back to the places they used to go around to every day with their masters. Well, you know . . . people . . . I mean, we're not that different."

"Jesus," Mrs. Sforza said.

"Aaaa, Mike's not taking it the wrong way. He understands."

His wife glanced over to make sure, then looking at him pointed her finger at her temple and spun it round and round.

Mr. Sforza continued: "And soon we'll be gone too - the last connection with your father. Look," he said before his wife reacted, "I'm only saying what's true. That's the way life goes. Did I ever tell you about the time your father attempted suicide?"

Mrs. Sforza spun away from the table. "Jee-zus!" She said it to her husband but she was looking at me. "We invite the guy over for lunch and you -"

"Waidda minute, waidda minute," Mr. Sforza said. He was unflappable. "That's what they thought. He would never commit suicide, your father."

"Who's 'they'?" I asked.

"The police at the scene."

A laugh exploded from Mrs. Sforza. "That!" Suddenly she looked very happy.

"You serious?" I asked.

"If you mean is it a true story, yes. Your father was driving to Newark early one Sunday morning - you know, one of those days when there isn't a car on the Pulaski Skyway. It must have been about six in the morning and it was summertime and beautiful out and he was crossing the Hackensack River when he got this sudden urge to stop at the edge of the roadway - just park the car and get out. There was nothing but empty highway as far as he could see in either direction and he figured it was safe, so he did. He leaned over the railing and looked down at the river."

"This is good," Mrs. Sforza said to me. She was looking very happy.

"Usually you hardly ever see a patrol car, especially on a Sunday morning and especially that early in the morning. But wouldn't you know it, just at that moment some state troopers or something come by and stop and one of them goes over to see if your father's okay and your father says, sure I'm okay, I was just admiring the view. The cop looks at him and says he'd better go admire it someplace else and never to try parking in the middle of a highway again. He said because there was no traffic he'd let him go this time. 'No problem,' your father said but he just stood there hoping they'd go away so he could take another look at the river. So the trooper says, 'Come on, come on, let's go. First you go, then we leave. I don't want no suicide on my hands.' So your father laughs. 'No, no,' he says. 'I'm a happy man, I'm enjoying life.' You know how your father talked -- the way people from Campobass' talk - we don't waste words."

"He wasn't from Campobass'," Mrs. Sforza said. "He was Calabres'."

"He wasn't from Campobass' but he had a cousin or something from Campobass' on his mother's side. So anyway, they all got in their cars and took off. Your father said the

Hackensack River looked really very beautiful from way up there."

"Yeah, look at it from ground level some time," Mrs. Sforza said. "Especially Jersey City. Jesus."

Mr. Sforza filled our glasses and said he knew it sounded crazy but nowadays he felt happiest with the memories of dead friends. Like my father.

"Which is not surprising. When you get to be our age, practically the only friends you have are all dead." He said he sometimes wished he was a believer so he could say prayers for certain people, but if you don't believe, you don't believe. "And at seventy-four you don't get converted too easy. Clara here gave up on me long ago. She told me I'm going straight to hell and not to bother to pass Go and collect my two hundred dollars. Which makes me laugh."

"Why?"

"Well, I mean, she would be absolutely right except that there's no such place as hell. But try to tell her that."

"There's no proof," Mrs. Sforza said. "You got proof?"

"Nobody believes in hell anymore," I agreed. "A lot of people still believe in heaven, though. Funny."

"Heaven!" he said with a laugh. "Right here is heaven. See that pear tree over there? That's heaven. This lunch is heaven and so is this wine. Here, let's have the rest of this heaven. Salut!"

He poured us each what was left in the bottle. I looked over at the spindly pear tree straining up from the cement. In a peripheral way I had always seen the tree but had never looked at it. It was a mass of withered branches and six plump pears: there were so few leaves left you could see all six pears at a glance. In contrast to the aged appearance of the tree, the pears looked healthy and young, in fact gaudy, like expensive Christmas tree ornaments: big, round, handsome, each an emerald green with one pink cheek. They looked like they were posing for a Gourmet photo spread on the beauty of orchard fruits.

Mrs. Sforza saw where I was looking and said: "They're crisp to bite into, not like those mushy yellow things you get in the supermarket. Of course with these teeth . . ."

"I'll bring one over when they're ripe," Mr. Sforza said. "You don't pick them. You wait for them to fall because that's when they have the most taste. But sometimes I help them fall. You give them a tap and see if they drop. This bunch doesn't have far to go."

He got a long bamboo pole that had been leaning against the house, walked over to the pear tree and probed through the scrawny branches. With the tip of the pole he nudged one of the pears, gently bumping its stem so as not to bruise the fruit or break off the thin twiggy branch it hung from. On the third poke the pear suddenly plummeted past his cheek and thudded on the cement.

"Here," he said, picking up the pear and bringing it over, "try that."

I took a bite.

He was smiling in anticipation. "Good, huh?"

"Delicious," I said. In fact it was. Luscious.

"What did I tell you?"

They observed me as I ate the pear - Mrs. Sforza, her head tilted back and leaned to one side, her bushy white eyebrows floating high up on her forehead as she enjoyed my pleasure, gazing at me with a fond look. I had to smile at the way she was looking, and when she saw me smile, her mouth spread into a grin.

I told them I had to think about going, that I had to catch a bus to New York to pick up some digital supplies.

"You don't have to go yet," Mr. Sforza said.

"This isn't exactly my last visit," I said. "About that suicide - when was that?"

"Let's see, that must have been around the end of the eighties, I think it was nineteen eighty-eight or eighty-nine. Were you born yet? Sit down."

"I was born in nineteen eighty."

"Listen, sit down. Yeah, your brother Pete -- rest in peace -- was around then but you weren't born yet. Your mother and father were practically newlyweds. Pete was about three months old when your father tried to commit suicide."

"The Pulaski Skyway," I said. I tried to visualize the scene of my father leaning over the railing a couple of hundred feet above the river.

"Right over the Hackensack River - not the Passaic River, the Hackensack. Take a look as you go by some time and you'll see where your father got stopped by the cops. Listen, stay put for a while. We're not finished yet."

"Jersey City cops," Mrs. Sforza said.

"Jersey City cops, Hoboken cops, Newark cops - cops are cops," Mr. Sforza said.

"Cops are cops, all right," she said. "Listen, we have cheese cake for dessert" - Mrs. Sforza à la Groucho bouncing her eyebrows up and down: the smiling siren enticing me. "From Hansen's, made this morning. It's still warm."

"That's right. You can't go yet," Mr. Sforza said. "We have to eat the cheese cake."

"Well, Hansen's," I said - "can't refuse that. But then I have to go, really."

"Sure. We don't want to keep you," Mr. Sforza said, "but you're welcome to stay as long as you like."

His wife served a thin creamy wedge so quivering tall on the serving spoon it was structurally unsound. As she handed the plate across the table, the wedge fluffed over on its side. Nobody made cheese cakes as deep and light as Hansen's. She served her husband and herself smaller slices, laying them flat.

"We're pigging out," she said. "Retirement's living."

She had worked for years as a seamstress in a Jersey City dress factory and after seven years of retirement still couldn't get over the luxury of doing nothing.

"Mm - really good," Mr. Sforza said swallowing a mouthful.

"That Hansen's - really good stuff. With a cheese cake like this, it's all in the ingredients you use and the way you prepare them."

"How is that different from the rest of cooking?" his wife asked.

He laughed. "She's too smart for me. What are you going to New York for?"

"I need paper and inks. And they're a whole lot cheaper when you buy a lot of them at once."

"It must be a fascinating field to be able to do photography. What is this, a wedding assignment?"

I said the phone call that had delayed me was about a free-lance job for a series the Journal was doing on the changing suburbs.

"I gotta hand it to you Castellanos - all that talent. Our two boys, one's a building contractor and the other one runs a gas station."

"Two gas stations now," Mrs. Sforza said. "He's got two of them now."

"Listen," I said, "I wish I knew how to build a house. There's some repairs I need to have done."

"No, I don't mean that. They're both honest and they're both good family men."

"Well?" Mrs. Sforza said. "Isn't that what counts?"

"Sure, I'm not saying that -- no complaints, except that one's in Ohio and one's in Indiana. And when you want to see your grandchildren . . . But they're fine boys. Here, take some more cheese cake."

"Yeah, that's true," Mrs. Sforza said. "One's in Ohio and one's in Indiana. You have to drive all the way across Pennsylvania to get to Ohio. Jesus."

As Mrs. Sforza served me another piece of cake, just slightly smaller than the first, I watched a blue jay glide silently across the yard to a soft landing at the top of the pear tree. As the jay looked over at us the small branch it landed on dipped and swayed under its impact.

"Beat it!" Mr. Sforza yelled. He flailed his arms. The jay soundlessly took off. "They're very loud birds," he explained. "Once they start jabbering and squawking. . . . I know they're only communicating with each other, but still."

"Yeah," Mrs. Sforza said. "Noisy goddam bastards."

I said, "Well, I really better be going. If I can move after this meal."

"We don't want to keep you, you understand. You sure you're okay healthwise? - eating properly?" Mr. Sforza said.

"You're not keeping me - and yes, I'm fine."

"Because we're like parents to you. Remember that."

"Campobass' people," Mrs. Sforza said to me, "they have this thing about health. They have to keep asking you if you're still healthy."

Feeling full hadn't spoiled my pleasure in putting away the second piece but now I felt heavy. As I cleaned off the plate I saw, over Mr. Sforza's shoulder, an old man appear in a backyard two or three houses down. He was with a little girl of about five or six, probably his granddaughter. She was leading him by the hand and taking giant steps and chanting. He was enjoying being with her. He trailed her loose-jointedly - or maybe he was pretending to be drunk. Or maybe an idiot.

"Ya-ya," he said.

"Ya-ya," she mimicked.

"Ya-ya," he repeated.

"Ya-ya," she said, laughing.

"Ya-ya."

"YA-YAAA," she yelled happily. Doing giant zigzagging steps, legs splayed out, she dragged him back inside, and the yard was quiet again.

"Ben Hanford," Mrs. Sforza said, "Ida's father. Haven't seen him in months."

"Retired fifteen years now," Mr. Sforza said. "Way back he used to work for the old Lehigh, I think, or the Lackawanna.

45

Bad diabetes."

"Why don't you go over and ask him how his health is doing?"

"He was named in some kind of bookkeeping scandal -- I forget. But he's a good man. He was crazy about his wife, poor thing, and you can tell he really loves his daughter and granddaughter."

"I like that story about my father," I said to Mr. Sforza.

"I knew you would," he said. "Can you imagine those cops thinking he'd jump in the river?"

"Listen, not to be impolite," Mrs. Sforza said, "but before we get back on the Pulaski Skyway again, I still have some house cleaning to do. See you, Michael," she said and gave a wave of her hand and disappeared into the kitchen.

As I was saying goodbye to Mr. Sforza we heard a vacuum cleaner start whining somewhere upstairs.

"Don't mind her," Mr. Sforza said. "It's senility, I think. But it could be the new false teeth. They're killing her."

The vacuuming sound stopped abruptly. Mrs. Sforza stuck her head out of a second-floor window. "Michael," she called down to me, "I don't want you to think I'm rude leaving like that. So, uh - good-bye," she said and slowly waved her arms from left to right as though we were a block apart.

"You weren't rude, Mrs. Sforza," I said waving back.

She flashed her teeth.

"How are you these days?" I said to Mr. Sforza.

"No point complaining. My father always used to say that people from Campobass' can take whatever happens in life. Like your father - well, he wasn't from Campobass' but he had a cousin there. Anyway, he almost went bankrupt once, back in the sixties, but he sprang back. You couldn't keep him down. Did he ever tell you about the Arizona land deal?"

"No."

"Maybe next time I'll tell you about that. Not even

bankruptcy could stop your father."

"It sounds like not even suicide could stop him," I said, smilimg.

Mr. Sforza laughed, jabbed my shoulder and yelled up: "Hey, Clara, did you hear that? Not even suicide could stop his father. If that isn't funny."

Mrs. Sforza looked at her husband and tapped her temple.

"Aaaa," her husband said. "She gets that way. I tell everybody it's her false teeth but I'm beginning to think it's her senility coming on."

"At least I've got the false teeth. What's your excuse?"

I went back to my house to pick up my checkbook and a few minutes later, as I headed for the bus to the Port Authority, I could hear Mr. Sforza clattering dishes and slamming pans into the sink and upstairs the vacuum cleaner whining away. Through the open kitchen door Mr. Sforza saw me taking the shortcut to the alley that ran behind the houses.

"Don't forget next time," he shouted from the doorway. "I'll tell you that story."

"What?"

"I'll tell you the bankruptcy story," he yelled.

The vacuuming stopped and Mrs. Sforza leaned her head out the window and not seeing me at first said to her husband, "What?"

Mr. Sforza stepped outside the doorway and looked up. "I said I love you," he said.

Mrs. Sforza flashed her teeth at him, then saw me at the back fence. She waved goodbye again. At her husband she tapped her temple and twisted her finger.

"Yeah, yeah, I know," Mr. Sforza said, beaming, "you love me too."

"Ha!" she said and continued her vacuuming.

About the Author

Hiag Akmakjian is the author of several fiction and non-fiction works, including the novels *30,000 Mornings* and *Cleo*.